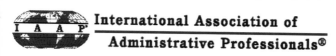

International Association of
Administrative Professionals®

Craig Hendricks
Fifth Third Bank
Compliments of Cincinnati Chapter October 2006
"Celebrating 60 Years of Administrative Excellence"
www.iaap-cinci.org

Jump!

Leaps In Organizational Performance & Teamwork

A Skydiver's Perspective

Craig,
Blue Skies.

David L. Hart

Jump Institute Inc

author·HOUSE™

1663 LIBERTY DRIVE, SUITE 200
BLOOMINGTON, INDIANA 47403
(800) 839-8640
WWW.AUTHORHOUSE.COM

First published by AuthorHouse 12/19/05

ISBN: 1-4208-8230-9 (sc)
ISBN: 1-4208-8231-7 (dj)

Library of Congress Control Number: 2005908201

Printed in the United States of America
Bloomington, Indiana

This book is printed on acid-free paper.

Cover Canopy Photo by: Michael McGowan
Cover Team Photo by: Norman Kent

Index of Landing Targets

Dedication

To My Family

Lori, Peter, Jacob, and Benjamin Hart

Acknowledgments

This project is the result of many people who provided their significant input and positive energy in the journey to publish this book. Truly a team effort.

Many thanks to Team Fastrax member Elisa Behnk for your unselfish and very useful feedback and editing. You challenged me to improve the message.

For providing feedback and content that directly contributed to the completion of this book, I am indebted to many critical readers, including but not limited to: Karen Ratliff, Linda Goeppner, Lisa Francis, Brace Barber, Brian Huseman, John Derosalia, and Helen Fahey.

For the inspiration to write this book and communicate the power of competition skydiving, thank you Team Fastrax, especially teammate Niklas Hemlin and my friend Dan BC; our conversations around high-performance teamwork allowed me to thoroughly explore and relate skydiving to life and business.

Most notable, to my wife Lori and my brother John, thanks for believing. Without your support none of this would be possible.

Foreword

Brace Barber, Author of No Excuse Leadership: Lessons from the U.S. Army's Elite Rangers

"Take one hour—no less—and concentrate solely on your personal life goals. Write them down. There should be some big and scary goals in there; then commit to achieving them. When you're done, if you've got anything worthwhile on the paper, you'll be exhilarated and scared."

I landed in the greenest field you've ever seen. The grass was long and bent over with dew. I didn't feel the slight chill in the air as I stood for a second in disbelief and in pure exhilaration. This kind of emotion only comes from the accomplishment of the extraordinary. It is an emotional state I believe everyone is striving for. I was enthusiastic to be alive. I believed I could take on the world and win. I was happy.

This sensation was all the result of the best business decision I've ever made, and it is something you can nearly duplicate in the next sixty minutes. The way to achieve this feeling is 100 percent safe. It's drug free, low cost, and guaranteed to get you a better job and income. There is a pattern to these decisions that you can develop into a habit and change your life. Apply this pattern to your organization and see productivity soar while the competition watches in amazement. There are risks to this pattern of decision making. Due to these perceived risks, only a small fraction of people will ever even take the first step.

For those of you who are willing, David Hart shows you how and why you must, for yourself and your team, accept the risks and create the habit of overcoming them. An important part of what David does is separate the complicated and dynamic world of organizations into their component pieces and make it understandable. You'll look into teamwork, training, hiring, vision, innovation, and more. You'll gain a perspective on how they work together and the important questions you need to ask yourself in order to enhance every area.

Only seconds before my parachute delivered me to that wonderfully solid field, I had voluntarily left the relative safety of a helicopter flying at 7,500 feet. I had thrown myself out of the open door and into the sensory-encompassing atmosphere of nothing. Though I was only eighteen years old and a cadet at West Point at the time, it was the best business decision I have ever made. It was not important because it made me a lot of money, but because it set a pattern for the decisions I've made throughout my life that have led to the success I enjoy now. What is that pattern? That is what David shows you in the context of business and life.

How can you enjoy that same exhilaration in the next sixty minutes? Take one hour—no less—and concentrate solely on your personal life goals. Write them down. There should be some big and scary goals in there; then commit to achieving them. When you're done, if you've got anything worthwhile on the paper, you'll be exhilarated and scared. With this exercise, you've already started the pattern; now let David help you achieve those goals.

So there I stood. Cow patties were randomly spaced around me as obstacles; first, to dissuade me from landing in this space to begin with; and second, to hinder my exit from the field should I find myself there. Only a few feet away, twenty cows were lined up, staring at me the way cows do. They were like the people who didn't understand my need to overcome limiting beliefs or the methods I used to do it. They just stood there with blank, uncomprehending eyes. They lived all their days fenced in that field.

David Hart has a parachute for you—Enjoy!

Brace E. Barber

[Author of *No Excuse Leadership: Lessons from the U.S. Army's Elite Rangers*. Leading expert in Immersion leadership and teamwork training. Leading Concepts, Inc.]

Introduction

Business is Like Skydiving

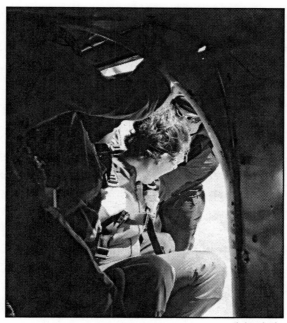

John Judy

A free-fall videographer hangs onto the outside of the aircraft as a tandem student prepares to take the leap with David Hart of Team Fastrax.

Look Within … Leap Beyond

Close your eyes and envision yourself standing on the threshold of an open aircraft door over two miles above the earth. The cool, turbulent air thunders inside the plane as you peer over the edge down through the mixture of blue sky and clouds to the patchwork of ground below. As you prepare to take the leap, you look within yourself and are confronted by the intense anxiety of the unknown.

Are you fully prepared and trained? Was your parachute packed properly? Will you actually summon the courage to jump from the airplane? Can we draw parallels from this experience to business? Is your organization facing significant challenges and obstacles? Are you and other co-workers required to step outside your comfort zone, to drive innovation and improvement? Does any of this sound familiar?

Perception is reality

Before we examine the many powerful parallels between business and skydiving, let's look at the activity itself for a moment. For the average person, jumping from an airplane appears to be sheer madness. The roots of this very commonly held perception are derived in part from the biplane barnstorming days of the early 1900s, when daredevils jumped from these WWI aircraft and promoters sensationalized it as a death-defying activity to draw larger crowds.

This perception was and still is reinforced every time a newspaper runs an article about another crazy skydiver who is seriously injured or killed in this seemingly reckless activity. The average person laments the apparent lack of even average intelligence it must take to call this activity a sport. It appears that every skydive is a fateful flip of the coin between life and death.

It's All Relative

A few statistics for you to consider: Each year there are over two million sport skydives conducted in the United States. Of these jumps, on average there are typically fewer than thirty fatalities reported annually to the United States Parachute Association. In fact, there were only twenty-one in 2004. A fraction of these involve first-jump students; the large majority come from experienced skydivers. Based on these figures, the odds of you making one of the annual two million jumps and being involved in a fatal incident is roughly 1 in 66,667.

Compare to other activities
Contrast these facts with your average commute to and from work and the possibility that you might be involved in a car accident resulting in serious injury or death. Further, consider how often you are confronted with automobile accidents in the newspaper, on TV, or even as you drive by in the perceived safety of your own car. According to U.S. DOT statistics, there are on average over six million automobile crashes every year in the United States; three million involve injured persons and result in more than 40,000 fatalities.

Watch your step
In a 2002 study released by the U.S. National Safety Council (NSC) titled "What Are the Odds of Dying?" the NSC determined that you have a 1 in 77 chance of expiring in a transportation accident in the average human life span. More surprising, you have a 1 in 229 chance of killing yourself by slipping, tripping, or stumbling. We sometimes joke to our skydiving students that the last step is a long one, but even the short ones we take for granted have very real risks associated with them.

It's human nature to maintain false perceptions

Because we have been so immersed in the imagery and frequency of automobile accidents, we have become either numb to it or we accept it as a necessary risk of daily life. I have been parachuting for over twenty years and have accumulated thousands of jumps; I have never had a broken bone for any reason. The odds are heavily in your favor to make at least one skydive and survive unscathed. I know this is all very morbid, but I have to confront you with the hard facts.

My point is not really to convince you to skydive as much as to question whether your current perceptions are holding you back.

This is important because we as humans have a tendency to fabricate our own reality. If we are going to drive increases in organizational performance and teamwork, we must first open our minds to new performance-enhancing opportunities. These opportunities cannot be discovered and exploited with a closed mind and narrow perceptions.

Perception is Reality

It has often been said, "Perception is Reality." If you perceive skydiving to be a high-impact and dangerous activity, I propose a change from your perception to the "real" reality. The reality is this: skydiving is not as safe as bowling or channel surfing, but it is certainly as safe as driving your car in rush-hour traffic. Again, I ask you to question the limiting beliefs and perceptions that are holding back both you and your organization.

Knowledge is power

Many individuals and business professionals have gone tandem skydiving with Team Fastrax and, as a result, their perception of the sport has been significantly altered for the better. They came to realize that the equipment is actually very reliable and has many built-in redundancies, the instructors are highly trained and competent, the parachute openings are not painful, and landings are most often quite soft. They are also quite surprised to find out how intense and disciplined competition skydiving is.

Don't misunderstand; while it is certainly far from the norm, people can be seriously injured or worse. People of all ages have made the leap, from younger than nine years to older than ninety years. The bottom line is this: we can't allow our own false perceptions to hold us back within our organizations.

Limiting Beliefs

This brings me to my passion of overcoming limiting beliefs and facing challenges head-on. Skydiving teaches this lesson like no other activity. We all have baggage that we carry with us that holds us back personally, in our organizations and in our relationships with others. Great inventions and discoveries come from open minds and a general dissatisfaction with the status quo.

Ben Franklin, a founding father of the United States and an inventor, made many great inventions and contributions to society. His failures by far outnumbered his successes, but he understood this as a requirement for creating innovative ideas. Thomas Edison realized a thousand failures before he discovered an effective filament for the light bulb. Even Walt Disney went bankrupt in his first business venture. What these highly successful people did not do was allow their failures to hold them back from achieving their goals. In fact, they used them as a learning tool to help them leap forward.

Training elephants

There is a well-known phenomenon in elephant training: early in a baby elephant's life it is chained to a sturdy tree. The baby elephant fights this bondage; yet over years, the elephant gives up and as an adult maintains the limiting belief that this same small chain can restrain it. The reality is that it could easily break the chain and free itself.

What is holding you back?

What limiting beliefs are ingrained in you and your corporate culture? What holds you back from taking the courageous jumps required to be a great company? Consider the companies that attain greatness and stay there. A culture of innovation and opportunity permeates these organizations. Limiting beliefs serve only one counterproductive purpose—to limit our accomplishments.

Apollo 13

A great example of an organization that used teamwork to successfully confront limiting beliefs was the historic effort by NASA to save the crew of the *Apollo 13* on their mission to land on the moon. In April 1970, Jim Lovell and the crew of the space capsule are hurling through space hundreds of thousands of miles from earth.

One thing after another goes wrong with the mission, and each time the space and ground crew confront the challenges head-on to come up with creative solutions to solve each problem. At one point during the mission they had to design a new air-filtration system out of various spare parts. To the outside observer this appeared to be a hopelessly impossible task, but they put their heads together and created a system that worked, and saved the lives of the crew. Imagine the power of overcoming limiting beliefs in this type of situation.

Real people with real challenges

Consider these real-life stories. Eric Weihenmayer is an adventure-sport athlete and has successfully climbed the seven highest mountains in the world, and skydives as well—completely BLIND.

Dana Bowman, former U.S. Army Golden Knight, was involved in a terrible skydiving accident that tragically killed his teammate and severed both his legs. Dana rehabilitated himself back onto active-duty status with the army skydiving team.

Dan Brodsky Chenfield was taking off in a plane with his skydiving team when it crashed into the ground, killing sixteen of the twenty-three people on the plane. He broke his neck and ended up in a coma for six weeks. Dan rehabilitated himself to compete again and went on to become a national and world champion, the Michael Jordan of competitive skydiving. Any one of these skydivers could have allowed their tragic circumstances to severely limit their future accomplishments, but they did not.

Organizational Effectiveness

Key landing points

Here are key drivers and competencies of organizational effectiveness and high-performance results. It is imperative to our success that we step outside our comfort zone and continually strive for personal and organizational effectiveness in these areas:

Teamwork

Innovation

Vision, Goals, and Action Plans

Supporting Cultures

Recruiting

Turnover and Retention

Training and Coaching

Leadership

Confronting Challenges

Relating to skydiving

Nearly every aspect of skydiving has some related tie-in to these key factors that enhance our personal success and that of our organizations.

Our vision is similar to the location from which we decide to exit the airplane; where we exit the plane has a great deal to do with whether we will land on target or not. Clearly communicating a shared vision can ensure that everyone collectively lands on target.

Parachute landing targets are analogous to the goals we set. Long- and short-term goals challenge and stretch us to explore our collective boundaries.

Our ability to drive innovation is not unlike the courage required to jump from an airplane and leap outside our comfort zones. This courage breeds a willingness to continue in the face of setbacks and failures.

We can relate the components of a parachute to our co-workers, departments, various locations, and divisions. As with the long rectangular cells that must be inflated for the parachute to operate properly, the people we work with must all work together to function properly and enable us to land on target.

The suspension lines of the parachute connect the skydiver to the parachute; broken suspension lines can cause serious flight problems. The suspension lines of our organizations are the primary aspects of a healthy culture of trust, accountability, commitment, effective communication, initiative, and preparation.

The obstacles we confront in our daily activities correspond to the wind, buildings, and power lines with which a skydiver must contend; some are predictable and some are not. The changing global economy and economic pressures are some of the major challenges we face daily. Our ability to effectively overcome these and other challenges will determine the long-term viability of our organizations.

Finally, the people we hire and promote within your organizations are, in effect, the people who pack our parachutes every day. Their performance directly affects whether the corporate parachute will open, function properly, and allow us to land on target. The fact is that we are all packing each other's parachutes every day in our families, work units, and social circles and we all have a cumulative positive or negative effect on each other.

Jump Institute

To reach the Jump Institute laboratory and classroom, you must first ascend nearly two miles and then provide 100 percent of your attention. The lessons presented in this book have been proven through trial and error over the years. Like the student skydiving manual, this book presents fundamental principles that may be ignored at one's own peril.

The information may at times seem fundamental to some, and yet revolutionary, enlightening, and inspiring to others. It is important to remember that at any time we are all susceptible to becoming trapped in our daily routines and habits. We can find it difficult to see outside the forest that surrounds us and find solutions to the obstacles that confront us.

Using This Book

The information in this book is highly interrelated; sections are interdependent to achieve true synergy and maximum effectiveness, and each chapter contains a useful alternative and insightful perspective on organizational effectiveness and teamwork.

I encourage you to release your mind like an opened parachute and welcome a new perspective: look within yourself and see things through the eyes of a skydiver. If this book is effective, it will stoke the fire of passion within you and inspire you to take courageous jumps within your organization.

Courageous questions
Look within yourself and your organization and leap beyond where you are right now. Take a moment at the end of each section and reflect on these questions alone or with other people. These questions will cause you to consider where you are now and where you want to be in the future. They can be the catalyst for you to open your mind to a whole

new perspective so you can confidently exit the plane with a successful JUMP!

Why skydiving as a metaphor?

Parables, fables, and allegories involve characters facing a dilemma or making a decision, and then dealing with the consequences of their choices. In addition to providing guidance and suggestions for action in life, they offer a metaphorical language that allows people to discuss difficult or complex ideas more easily. Our willingness to leap from a story example to a general guiding principle makes the use of parables, fables, and allegories a powerful learning tool. Skydiving as a metaphor is so potent because many of the functions and tasks are critical and extremely time-sensitive, the way business functions and tasks ought to be

Teamwork

The Team Fastrax Story

Lisa Flory

The Team Fastrax project
Demo/Tandem, 4-Way, and Canopy Pilot Teams

Why do we as humans enjoy athletic endeavors so much? Our interest often surpasses the casual entertainment value into the realm of obsession. Professional football fans go to the extreme of painting their bodies in team colors and exposing their bare skin to the below-freezing weather of the football season. Athletes in any endeavor who show persistence and determination in the face of overwhelming odds and achieve success tap right into the main artery of our emotional bloodstream. They lift us up and inspire us: just look at the great movies such as *Rudy, Rocky, Vision Quest,* and sports documentaries such as the success story of the U.S. Olympic gold medal hockey team of 1980.

Competitive Skydiving

I personally enjoy team sports where a group of athletes are training to achieve something better than average. This, in part, drove me to compete at the U.S. Nationals several times in formation skydiving, and it gives me a unique inside perspective on the sport. A common question people ask me is, "What's the sport in skydiving?" People seem to think, "If you live, you win," and the majority of the population is simply not educated about what is involved to become a top athlete in the sport.

As an athletic discipline, competitive skydiving requires as much focus, determination, and athletic ability as just about any other sport. To understand competitive four-way formation skydiving, imagine the precise timing required for synchronized swimming combined with the anticipation of swing dancing. Then get a good grip on three other people and leap out of a plane together at 10,500 feet. Now you have a very fundamental understanding of the dynamics involved.

Four of the team members fly their bodies to build various formations required to score points, while one person hovers above the other four with a helmet-mounted video camera to document it. The judges watch the first thirty-five seconds from the time the team leaves the plane and they award one point for every successful formation built. The team with the most points at the end of the meet wins. On a fast sequence, also called a draw, a top team can transition from one formation to the next in less than a second, scoring thirty-five to forty points in thirty-five seconds.

If this all sounds confusing, imagine attempting to execute this at 120 mph, knowing in the back of your mind that you have to activate your parachute at some point. This sport requires nothing less than disciplined, intense focus.

Balance is Critical

As in all aspects of a balanced life, skydiving requires that the needs of the individual be balanced with the needs of the team. To understand this more completely, compare skydiving to other sports and organizational issues.

Similar to running hurdles in track, formation skydiving requires that you fly your body quickly, yet remain in control. Moving so quickly that you lose control soon reaches the point of diminishing returns. Do you want your tax accountant to work as fast as possible, or as fast as they can and still perform competently? How many errors can a bank teller afford to make? Or a brain surgeon? At the same time, his or her time is very expensive, so they must be efficient.

Like playing the position of a wide receiver in football, skydiving demands that you are focused on catching the ball yet are aware of the other players around you. In our organizations we must be focused on our own performance yet still be aware of how effectively we are interacting with our co-workers. Being 100 percent aware of everything around you typically means you are the person who complains at the water cooler. Conversely, being 100 percent focused on yourself means you probably have no idea if you are effectively interacting with your co-workers.

Finally, formation skydiving requires that your nerves are like those of a golfer in order to be relaxed yet ready. Successful teams must balance their own individual efforts with the needs of the team to achieve optimum performance. Being 100 percent relaxed tends to lead to complacency. On the flip side, it is impossible to maintain a state of 100 percent readiness. Better to manage your energy and focus it at the best time. All this makes these the critical elements to balance:

Quick & Controlled
Focused & Aware
Relaxed & Ready

The Birth of Team Fastrax

Team Fastrax is currently one of the top performing skydiving teams in the world. It was initially formed in 2002 with relatively inexperienced skydiving competitors. The team debuted at the 2003 U.S. Nationals, where the team showed a remarkable ability to accelerate the learning curve to a very respectable level of performance in less than twelve months. Not an unheard-of feat, but certainly rare. I was part of that first-year team, along with John Hart, Bob Akers, Niklas Hemlin, and videographer Kip Loemiller.

All of us on the initial team were married with children, the average age being close to forty. Most were pursuing professional careers outside skydiving. There were many reasons (excuses) why the project shouldn't have even started. What we all had in common, though, was a passion for competitive skydiving and a mutual commitment to maximizing the use of our time, energy, and resources in an effort to achieve significant performance gains in competitive skydiving.

Maximizing resources

To achieve this breakthrough performance, the team collected over seventy hours of body flight in vertical wind tunnels, 650 skydives, and countless hours of ground training in preparation. Our team pulled in key resources when needed, including a sports psychologist, yoga instructor, and sports nutritionist. The actual training sessions were intense and often somewhat grueling.

Because of our professional obligations, time was a limiting factor. Often the team would make twenty-five or more training skydives a day for several days at a time. This training intensity was relatively unheard of and, unsurprisingly, drew criticism from other athletes and teams. Ultimately, it worked for Team Fastrax.

Lessons to learn

There are two lessons here. First lesson: It is human nature to resist change and what is not already a widely accepted principle. Second lesson: What works for one team or organization does not easily apply to another team or organization that may have a completely different culture and goals or may be in a different part of their performance cycle.

For example, you must be in peak mental and physical condition to make 100-plus four-way training jumps in three to four days, and to repeat that every other week for a year. Don't even attempt to go there if you're not fully prepared! It will be completely counterproductive and result in extreme frustration.

Similarly with organizations, just because we read a successful case study on XYZ Company doesn't mean that we can effectively incorporate the exact same methodology into our organization. Every team must go through a discovery process to develop a team vision, goals, standards, and norms that are uniquely applicable to them.

The 2004 Bronze Medal

Roster changes

The 2003 U.S. Nationals came and went that year, and the project continued, with the ultimate goal of winning the gold medal at the 2004 U.S. Nationals. A new lineup emerged with John Hart, Niklas Hemlin, Billy Andrews, Eric Gin, and videographer John Judy. Team member selection is critical, and these new team members were strong.

The team jumped right in and completed nearly 1,000 training jumps, in addition to a substantial dose of wind-tunnel training and countless hours of ground training and physical fitness. It all paid off in the fall when the team surprised everyone but themselves and won the bronze medal at the 2004 U.S. Nationals. The project continues.

Results of the 2005 Nationals

A record-breaking eighty teams registered for four-way formation skydiving at the 2005 U.S. Nationals. Of these eighty teams, at least six very competent Open Class teams were capable of winning a medal. These factors would set the stage for the most competitive nationals in the history of the sport and seriously challenge Team Fastrax, the returning 2004 bronze-medal champions.

After ten rounds of skydiving, and one jump-off round, Team Fastrax finished in fifth place. As heartbreaking as shortfalls in performance results can be, there are always lessons to be learned that we can apply to our future benefit.

Overnight success

After viewing the disappointing results, someone said to me, "It only takes ten years to achieve overnight success." Meaning, keep a long-term perspective on performance results. In effect, the 2005 performance becomes part of the relatively young team's long-term learning curve. Therefore, it is beneficial to take a long-term perspective on performance results.

Competition is a given

As hard as Fastrax trained for the 2005 Nationals, so did many other teams. In effect, there is no sleep for the wicked. Our global economy reflects this fact quite clearly. There are many domestic and foreign organizations working hard to raise the bar, providing new and innovative business solutions to compete with our own existing products and services. To combat this, we can encourage a culture of innovation and continuous improvement.

The Team Vision

The ultimate vision of Team Fastrax is to strive for greatness and maximum synergy in order to achieve peak performance, likely leading to the highest measure of success as gold-medal recipients at the national and world level.

The entire Team Fastrax four-way and canopy-pilot competition teams, precision-demonstration jump, and public-relations tandem teams share this winning behavior and pursuit of excellence. Regardless of roster changes over the years, the vision is driven by the same focused efforts to give 100 percent to the team goals, and through relentless efforts to continually drive improvements in performance.

Like world-class swimmers at the highest level, fractions of a second in execution can mean the difference between a gold medal and no medal at all. The team must consistently pursue every practical performance-enhancing option possible and, at the same time, maintain the discipline required for consistent and effective training, day after day, week after week, month after month, and year after year in pursuit of the team vision.

Corporate Teamwork

Jim is vice president for a Fortune 500 distribution company and understands the interdependency and need for teamwork within his division. Every person within the organization must work together to provide the price, service, and quality required to remain viable in an extremely competitive and mature industry.

Initially the sales representative brings the account on board, after which there is an ongoing collaborative effort to effectively maintain and grow the client's business. Customer service people take the orders. The purchasing department ensures inventory is available. The warehouse pulls the proper item and loads the truck, after which a driver ensures that the product arrives in a timely manner.

Ultimately, we have many other people and departments that touch our clients on any given transaction. It is a constant challenge to ensure that every person knows he or she has a very real impact on our ability to remain profitable and competitive. The ability to communicate and operate collaboratively is a critical competency.

Peak Performance Comes From Within

Like a healthy regimen of food, exercise, and sleep, it is imperative that we constantly feed our minds with new and alternative perspectives on performance management and organizational effectiveness.

My experiences as an Army Ranger, competitive skydiver, and entrepreneur combine to give me a unique perspective on group effectiveness. However, I am constantly exposing myself to alternative perspectives in my quest for personal and professional enlightenment. Skydiving teams change their action plan as they mature over time, ultimately developing a unique system that works best for them.

Your organization
Competitive skydivers train hard to overcome obstacles and build competencies to reach maximum synergy and peak performance. We can do the same within our organizations; we just need to take the proverbial leap. It is never easy to increase organizational effectiveness and teamwork. There is no "silver bullet" or "pill" you can take; it requires focused and meaningful communication and passionate action over time.

Keys to Making the Jump

🪂 An effective team and the individuals within it must balance the elements of being quick yet controlled, focused yet aware, and relaxed yet ready.

🪂 It is human nature to resist change, so it pays to develop a team culture that encourages open-minded thought. This is more conducive to driving high-performance results.

🪂 Every group of people is different. Change one person on a team and the group dynamics change. What works for one group may not work for another without some modifications.

Courageous Questions

🪂 What level of interpersonal synergy and teamwork is required to achieve peak performance? Try to think in terms of specific and measurable competencies needed to achieve your goals.

🪂 Are you committed to doing what it takes to make this happen? Commitment means dedicating the time, energy, and resources to make meaningful and lasting changes.

🪂 How will you address the strengths, weaknesses, obstacles, and threats that exist with individuals in your organization that need to be constructively confronted—organizationally and individually?

Leaps in Innovation

Driving Change, Improvement, and Creativity in Organizations

*Gene Newsome of Team Fastrax flying a
very large U.S. flag into an event.*

Competition and the rapidly expanding global economy are accelerating the need for increased levels of organizational efficiency and innovation. At the same time, trust in corporate leadership is close to an all-time low. The deterioration of trust is in part driven by the colossal corporate debacles involving such titans as Enron, Tyco, and other high-profile companies exhibiting leadership "indiscretions." The full engagement of the workforce will be a requirement for organizations to survive and prosper in this challenging and changing environment. Management has much work to do in overcoming this atmosphere of distrust.

Leadership

The ability of organizations and teams to be innovative is critical to landing on target and sustaining high performance. Effective leadership has a role in achieving a culture of trust, ensuring that employees are confident that their parachutes will open, and encouraging a willingness to take innovative leaps.

Some level of risk is nearly always associated with innovation, and a basic level of trust is the most critical element allowing people to take risks. In order to create a culture of innovation an effective leader will encourage elements of dissatisfaction, recognition, and play within the organization.

Encourage dissatisfaction

Great products, services, and inventions come out of some form of human dissatisfaction. However, most people are comfortable with the status quo and are, in fact, uncomfortable with change and risk. Create an environment where employees feel passionate about finding alternative and more effective solutions to obstacles and challenges. Encourage an environment of dissatisfaction.

Give recognition
Take the time to provide positive reinforcement, which encourages creative thinking, initiative, and risk taking. This is counterintuitive to corporate America's predominant risk-averse orientation and lack of tolerance for errors and mistakes.

Encouraging playfulness
Experimentation and exploration can be a great deal of fun. Every breakthrough in human body flight has typically been a result of jumpers playfully experimenting with different orientations in free fall; the results of individual and group play expand what we are able to collectively accomplish in groups. Encourage an environment of playful experimentation in your organization.

Risk and Innovation

There is a direct correlation between risk and innovation; we can look at nearly every great discovery and see some level of risk. In all aspects of human achievement, those who step up to champion innovations are the true pioneers of positive change. I have often reflected upon the tremendous risks the pioneers of our sport assumed to improve skydiving safety and performance.

Early pioneers
In the early 1900s it was widely believed that a person would pass out from even the briefest period of free fall. On April 28, 1919, Les Irvin disproved this by performing the first intentional free-fall jump from an airplane at McCook Field in Dayton, Ohio. After this discovery, it became widely believed that it was impossible to free-fall in a stable body position. (Up to this point skydivers would tumble out of control in a fetal position.)

In 1947, Frenchman Leo Valentin pioneered the highly stable, spread-eagle Valentin Position, and soon thereafter, skydivers began holding onto each other in free fall, choreographing formations in the sky. Innovation continued to spur more innovation and, over time, the number of people in the formations increased.

Breaking barriers
Free fall, canopy flight, and the equipment required to perform them have evolved to become very reliable and predictable. The resulting accessibility of the sport has been made possible by decades of risks and subsequent innovations.

Thirty relatively recent innovation of tandem skydiving has allowed people to skydive late into their lives. Former president Bush made his fifth parachute jump as a tandem skydive on his eightieth birthday; his first parachute jump was from his flaming aircraft over a Pacific island during World War II.

Consider the planning and risk evaluation required to establish the current world record for the largest free-fall formation, which took place in February of 2004 in Thailand— 357 skydivers linked in free fall at 120 mph. Much like Roger Banister breaking the four-minute-mile barrier, skydivers are always pushing the established "glass ceilings" in our sport.

Trust and Risk

Effective corporate cultures are built on a fundamental level of trust. This entails an environment where the workforce is willing to take chances without fear of negative repercussions, reprisals, and backlash. A foundation of trust cements the sense of corporate mission and shared expectation of integrity.

Effective communication and ethical business practices promote the generation of solutions and encourage the freedom to take risks. There can be no finger-pointing blame game or political tactics to avoid accountability.

An environment of trust encourages individual abilities to flourish and discourages the functional silos that isolate true potential. We can build a culture of trust by being trustworthy ourselves. To build trust and drive improvements with skydiving students, an effective jumpmaster uses proper communication, demonstration, and preparation.

Communication
Demonstration
Preparation

Encouraging Innovation

A large Midwest manufacturer of rebuilt engines and transmissions has an active Open-Door Policy that allows anyone, at any time, to call or walk into the office of a manager, People Department VP, or president and discuss any concerns, questions, etc. The door is always open and there are no negative repercussions. Every associate is given a business card that identifies phone extensions. Even the president's home phone number is provided.

Linda, director of the People Department, went on to explain: "We have an Advisory Committee that allows fifteen individuals to serve for eighteen months with three executives on a committee that meets monthly. They discuss questions, comments, concerns, rumors— anything they want—very candidly; management considers and makes decisions, which are then communicated to the workforce."

There is also a Continuous Improvement Program, where individuals come up with ideas. No idea is too small or dumb—all are at least considered and responded to and/ or acted upon. Individuals earn "Elmo Bucks" (equivalent to real dollars) for ANY idea, and then more for ideas that are implemented.

Communication

When communicated with properly, a student skydiver clearly understands what is expected and the implications of appropriate and inappropriate action. He or she is not left to fabricate a worst-case scenario based on unclear expectations.

Students visibly relax when it is explained that there is no pressure to perform a specific training objective (as long as their life does not depend on it; obviously, there are some things that are critical, like activating your own parachute). Once they realized it was okay to make some mistakes and experiment with their body flight, they progress much more quickly.

The same is true when Team Fastrax is pushing training performance levels. The more open the team is to alternative perspectives the more likely they are to seize upon performance-enhancing changes. This type of communication requires an effective feedback process, one that is built on respect and trust; one that allows for alternative perspectives.

Demonstration

In order for people to feel they can take risks, we must demonstrate by our actions that it is okay to take appropriate risks to drive innovation. This means we don't chastise people when they take a chance and fail. Often this goes counter to our need to minimize error. However, if we are consistent in our reinforcement, over time people around us will open up.

An effective skydiving instructor also clearly demonstrates prudent risk in his or her actions. It is a commonly known phenomenon that students will emulate experienced skydivers' good and bad behavior. Because of this it is critical that skydiving instructors, like business leaders, are constantly aware of this and demonstrate proper risk taking.

This begs the question of what is prudent risk. That is a very relative question. Ask a bank CEO and a research and development company and you will receive two very different answers. Ultimately, prudent risk is determined by the organizational vision and goals, and is demonstrated through the action of leadership.

Preparation
When a skydiving student feels properly prepared, he or she is more likely to relax and focus on improvement rather than obsess over whether he or she will perform the basic safety procedures. The same holds true in our work teams. If we give people the tools to succeed, they are apt to focus on driving powerful innovation.

Conflict and Egos

Okay, let's be honest: who really loves critical feedback? Nobody. The fact is, constructive feedback exists in most every high-performance culture.

The teams that achieve true synergy have a culture of trust that allows for brutally honest communication. This will mean that frequent confrontation is likely to take place. However, if the organization focuses on the driving vision of the group and takes the steps to build real trust, the team will identify opportunities and explore performance-enhancing ideas. Individual egos are minimized and downplayed, while the good of the team is put first.

Encourage Leaps

As in business, there are still very real risks in skydiving, but the risks of jumping are well managed; the resulting trust is a springboard for freedom, just as it is in life.

Where can we find examples of trust as a foundation of success? For my answer I look back to 1983—my first parachute jump at Fort Benning, Georgia. It was early on in my enlistment in the army and I was on the way to becoming an Army Ranger. The Army Jump School is three weeks long, with a history of extremely professional and safe operations dating back to World War II.

Appropriate tools and support

The leadership of the jump school has all the critical elements of a successful program in place. All the student needs to do is show up at the school, follow the curriculum, and perform when called upon to do so. In this case, no real innovation is required, just large amounts of trust, the critical element of a parachute jump.

This requires trust in the equipment, training, aircraft, weather, jumpmaster, and, most important, the ability to perform—much to contemplate at the door of your first jump, a moment of considered risk, to be sure. This moment of trust helped me to uncover my potential, find the joy of jumping, serve my country, and discover an ability to assume personal responsibility and take initiative to reach my goals.

Along with the other students, I moved on to four more exhilarating leaps from large cargo aircraft packed front to back with very nervous students. Together, as graduates, we shared the momentous award of the coveted silver jump wings. After graduation, some never jumped again, while some moved on to active-duty jump units such as the Rangers.

Take the Leap Now

It takes time to build trust and create a culture of innovation. The velocity of business consistently increases each day. Ensure that the parachute of trust is in place sooner rather than later. You can choose a culture of constructive dissatisfaction, positive reinforcement, recognition, and playful experimentation.

The leadership within every organization can drive innovation with the goal of a workforce permitted and encouraged to take acceptable risks. The risk and return payoff is usually proportional: the higher the risk, the higher the return.

Engage the workforce

Competition and a global economy necessitate an effective loop of input and feedback. Conflict managed constructively generates new ideas, and considered risk has become the very tool of survival. We can pack the parachute of our organization by effectively communicating expectations, demonstrating appropriate behavior through leading by example, and preparing people for success by providing the required tools, training, and coaching.

Empowered employees become partners in success; diversity is embraced to feed alternative perspectives, and management creates a shared vision and sense of purpose, operating ethically in all aspects of business and inspiring the workforce to do likewise. It is time to take the leap, jump out of our comfort zones, and create a culture of innovation.

Keys to Making the Jump

🦅 Establish a trust-based work environment that encourages dissatisfaction with the status quo.

🦅 Give appropriate recognition for risk taking.

🦅 Create a culture of playful experimentation.

🦅 Clearly communicate expectations and allow for an effective feedback process where the brutal facts can be constructively confronted.

🦅 Lead by example and demonstrate appropriate risk taking to drive creativity.

🦅 Take the time to prepare the team for success, giving the necessary training and tools to become innovative.

Courageous Questions

🦅 Can you openly share the brutal truth with your peers and co-workers? What exactly is impeding the creative process in your organization?

🦅 Are creative problem-solving and brainstorming ideas for the future encouraged and rewarded?

🦅 How much failure or risk are you willing to accept personally and within the organization to drive continuous improvement and innovation?

🦅 How will you improve upon the current status of trust and innovation?

Pick Your Spot, Land on Target

Exploring Organizational Vision, Goals, and Planning

John Hart

Team Fastrax lands on target at an NCAA football game demonstration jump.

We have all seen the positive results of vision. The United States was founded and developed based on a vision: that of living in a better, more prosperous place of fertile land and limitless wealth. Most of our great inventions are a result of a passionate vision for a better mousetrap, writing instrument, source of energy, or more efficient transportation. Having a vision that people "buy into" will drive a person or group to achievements that were previously thought impossible. How can we get our arms around this thing called Vision?

Vision—Spotting for Success

To a large degree, where you get out of an airplane determines where you can expect to land. In skydiving we call this spotting. A good business leader, like an effective spotter, considers many variables before making a decision about where to exit over the ground. To exaggerate the point, if you jump out of a plane over Ohio it's ludicrous to think you can land in California. Why should our organizations be any different? Having a well-defined vision will ensure that everyone exits the plane with the best opportunity to land on target.

Are you a good spotter?

Like the spotter who decides where a planeload of skydivers should exit the aircraft, organizational leaders play a key role in establishing and maintaining focus on the primary vision. Ultimately, if you don't have an effective vision, you shouldn't be at all surprised where you land. If you're lucky, you might land on target. But perhaps you allow the wind to carry you into power lines, trees, buildings, or water. Not at all pleasant landing areas! Establishing a clearly defined and articulated vision, you are more likely to achieve team "buy-in" and individual alignment with the related goals.

Dan Brodsky-Chenfield

I had the good fortune to spend a day in conversation with Dan Brodsky-Chenfield. Dan is affectionately known within the skydiving world as "BC." He happens to be one of the most successful athletes in the history of skydiving. Over the years Dan has accumulated scores of national and world championship medals in competitive formation skydiving.

The importance of proper preparation
While we were talking, Dan brought up the point that in four-way formation skydiving, the judges score the first thirty-five seconds of ten jumps to determine your total score for the meet. He noted the irony that a top skydiving team will spend literally thousands of hours of a training year preparing for those ten thirty-five-second intervals of competition.

A well-thought-out vision, goals, and action plan become part of the preparation required for an organization to be successful. In fact, preparation plays a critical role in all aspects of business.

A passion for excellence
Dan has spent literally decades training to prepare for skydiving competition. He is so passionate about his vision that after a plane crash that killed sixteen people and put him in a coma for six weeks, he fully recovered to continue training and competing. The fact is, on any given training jump a team may spend thirty to sixty minutes or more preparing for it. The ratio of preparation to competition is very lopsided; however, it is critical to success in any endeavor.

When the Going Gets Tough....

If jumping is the fun part, what drives an athlete to commit all that time and energy in intense preparation? Adequate preparation most often involves long hours of repetitious activity, day after day; countless hours are spent on physical, mental, and spiritual training.

When the onion is peeled back and you get down to the heart of what REALLY is driving all this commitment and passionate preparation, the motivating factors can vary greatly from one person to the next. What a great team has in common is a driving vision, a vision of what each person most desires at the heart of the onion. This is what gets each person out of bed early in the morning, prepared to attack the day with vigor.

High-performance organizations require the same commitment, specific goals, and a vision that everyone buys into. Without it, true peak performance is nearly impossible to achieve.

Ranger example

During my enlistment as an Airborne Ranger there were many moments of utter misery and complete exhaustion. There were times when I was cold, wet, sore, tired, and hungry down to the core of my body, with no hope of relief for days—only miles and miles of continued patrolling with a 100-pound rucksack in frigid swamp water with my fellow Rangers.

This Ranger experience (and intense athletic training) is an extreme example of deep commitment, when a mutually accepted, driving vision becomes critical—a vision that runs down to the deep core of personal motivation. Performance in life and business is directly tied to our level of commitment, which is directly tied to our ability to "tap into" a driving vision.

Prioritize Appropriately

What should come first: intense activity and preparation, or effective communication to determine the purpose and objective of the activity and preparation?

There is no doubt that great achievements are most often preceded by intense activity and preparation. However, how can you achieve a meaningful level of "buy in" from each individual before all the time, energy and money is invested? How many goals have people started only to flounder later after a significant amount of investment?

False expectations

As an example, after I had spent over a year as a private in the 1st/75th Ranger Battalion, I was selected to attend Army Ranger School at Fort Benning, Georgia. This school is intended to be the most intense and elite military leadership school in the world. I was amazed to see the number of students who either quit or dropped out the first seven days of the fifty-eight-day school.

Often these were soldiers who had no idea for what they had volunteered. By this I mean they knew Ranger School would be challenging, but they were not fully aware of just how challenging it would be. It wasn't always that they weren't physically prepared; more often, they did not mentally "buy into" the purpose. They had no strong driving vision burning brightly within them when the instructors once again asked us to crawl through the sawdust into the ice-cold, muddy worm pit.

Define the vision first, because it is the one thing you will come back to when the going gets tough.

Defining the Vision

So how do we define a vision for families, teams, organizations, and ourselves? It will help to first ask yourself this question: In the absence of detailed instructions or directives, what will guide your activities and response to challenges?

There is nothing more irritating than the customer service representative who responds to your request inappropriately or irrationally because it is company policy and who does not choose an effective solution that is seemingly right in front of him or her.

What is required are not more detailed instructions, but rather some broad guiding principles that can be applied to any situation. These are often detailed in a corporate vision and values.

A Vision Can Drive Action

What happens when there are major changes and shifts in an industry? How should organizations respond and what guides the response?

A well-established leader in the manufacture of classical pianos had to change or go out of business. Electronic musical instruments were significantly reducing the demand for classical pianos.

The corporate vision is to provide superior manufactured products and customer service to the world. It was decided that there would be a significant shift in the product offerings, a change that would complement the corporate vision and not change it. The new goals would fit well into the existing strengths of the organization.

As it turned out the company effectively mobilized its workforce to a highly successful shift into the office furniture industry and electronic products. They still fulfill their vision through focused goals and the related action plans, just with different products.

Goals—The Landing Target

If you want to hit the bull's-eye when parachuting, you obviously have to clearly identify where you want to land. This is equivalent to establishing well-defined and specific goals. I have conducted many high-profile demonstration jumps into NASCAR events, NCAA football games, and even symphony performances. In these circumstances, we have a specific target with very limited alternative landing areas. For example, if you don't land on the football field, your other landing options are the bleachers and stadium structure itself. Not pleasant options that certainly could hurt.

There is a simple acronym, **SMART**, which skydiving instructors use with first-time students when establishing training goals.

Specific
Measurable
Achievable
Relevant
Trackable

Specific

Make your goals specific and very clearly identify the intended target. If you want to increase this, decrease that, or accomplish anything, focus on the bull's-eye by leaving no ambiguity. For example, I might set a goal to spend twenty hours a week of quality time with my family. This would be a very specific goal.

Measurable

In order to make adjustments and stay on track, your goal needs to be measurable. If I do choose to spend eight hours a week with my children, this is easily measurable. Simply acknowledging that I need to spend more quality time with my children is too vague.

Achievable

Your goals must also be achievable. Is it realistic to think I might spend 100 hours a week with my family? I believe that is highly unlikely. It's okay to establish goals that will cause you to stretch a little, but don't set yourself up for failure by setting unrealistic goals.

Relevant

Your goals should be relevant. Is it relevant for me to spend quality time with my three boys? Absolutely! Is it relevant to you? Probably not!

Trackable

All your goals should be easily trackable so you can measure your progress and make adjustments to ensure success.

Planning—Establishing a Landing Pattern

We know that to land on target a jumper must first pick the appropriate location to exit the aircraft. Once we determine the vision and related goals, we then clearly define individual roles, objectives, and action required.

After successfully deploying the parachute, each skydiver must make decisions and adjustments "on the fly" to compensate for the constantly changing wind conditions. An experienced jumper uses his or her best judgment to make these corrections, without input from anyone else.

Like airline pilots, skydivers fly their parachutes in a very specific box pattern. Ideally, all the other jumpers fly the same directional pattern. The team lands on target more consistently, avoiding serious injury and hazardous collisions. This is teamwork at its best.

jump!

Keys to Making the Jump

🦅 Create a commonly shared Vision, Goals, and Action Plan. It is the one thing that people will come back to in the absence of external motivation.

🦅 To clearly define and articulate your goals and action plans use the acronym **SMART** as an outline. Set goals that are specific, measurable, achievable, relevant, and trackable.

Courageous Questions

🦅 When you peel back your onion, what motivates you to action?

🦅 Can you define the driving vision in your life?

🦅 Can you define the driving vision for your organization? Are your personal and professional visions and goals aligned?

🦅 Reflect on how your personal driving vision influences your role and activities within your organization.

Broken Suspension Lines Are a Malfunction

Exploring Organizational Culture

A Team Fastrax member pilots a parachute.

The Parachute—Laying the Foundation

A modern sport parachute is rectangular, composed of many long individual cells that open in the front. Imagine that each of the cells represents an organizational function, a teammate, or a family member. All the cells must be fully inflated for the parachute to function properly. If one or more cells are not functioning properly, the parachute will fly erratically or may not fly at all. So it is in life and business.

Teamwork
Like the cells of a parachute, we need each person pulling his or her weight to achieve our full potential. Now visualize the suspension lines that run from the canopy down to the jumper and connect the two together. If one or more of these suspension lines is broken, the canopy will not function properly and may not function at all. Think of these suspension lines connecting the canopy to the jumper's harness as representing the critical elements of organizational culture such as Trust, Preparation, Communication, Accountability, Initiative, and Commitment. Let's take a look at each of these critical elements.

Trust
Preparation
Communication
Accountability
Initiative
Commitment

Trust

Trust is such a crucial component of life. If we do not have it in others and ourselves, it is nearly impossible to consistently achieve our goals. Many factors contribute to establishing trust. Within our organizations, leadership plays a key role. How often have we been affected by the "do as I say, not as I do" leadership style?

My children are little sponges. They are more likely to duplicate my behavior than believe what I might say to them. Adults are no different. All of us must have trust in the leadership of our organizations. The synchronization of action and words builds trust.

Confidence plays a crucial role in establishing trust. Fear of the unknown, conflict, and failure can have a huge impact on a company culture and the related results achieved. Critical and meaningful discussions are nearly impossible in a state of fear and low confidence. To build trust, we should take steps to encourage confidence in each other and in the leadership of our organizations.

Preparation

Would you jump from an airplane without proper preparation? Obviously, you wouldn't. Nor are you going to complete the grueling Hawaiian Iron Man Triathlon without conducting the proper preparation.

Life and business are no different. If we are thrown into an intense situation where expectations are high, we pay the price if we do not thoroughly prepare. In skydiving, neglecting to prepare can have fatal consequences. Poor preparation in the Iron Man means failure, as it can in business.

Start with the basics and be systematic about preparation. Give people the proper training and tools to prepare for success. By doing this, we minimize errors and increase efficiency.

Pre-jump preparation

On a typical Team Fastrax training day, the team has very specific objectives and a system for proper preparation; this ensures the most productive day possible. These training sessions entail a constantly evolving system that is enhanced and improved upon depending on where the team is in their learning curve.

A young team will often make the fundamental mistake of poor jump preparation, virtually ensuring a weak performance in training and competition. The second mistake that new teams commonly make is to attempt advanced training that they do not yet have the collective capability to perform. This results in frustration and, again, poor results. To prepare like Team Fastrax, organizations should consider progressing one step at a time and resist the temptation to skip critical steps on the path to advanced levels of performance.

People are commonly blown away by the fact the team can make thirty or more effective training jumps in a day for several consecutive days. However, it is important to note that the team didn't start at this point. Extensive training, experience, and preparation led up to that increased level of performance.

Communication

In order to have a safe and effective skydive, all communication with first-time jumpers must be accurate and complete. It is essential that this is done in a manner that ensures a real understanding of the key goals, the related plan, and how each person fits into it. Most important is their ability to execute appropriate action when required. Poor communication can lead to catastrophic consequences in skydiving. In the worst-case scenario, skydiving students do not clearly understand what is required of them and they are not able to execute the required action in an emergency.

Verbal and non-verbal communication plays a huge role in how people respond to us. If we desire an organization of continuous improvement, we have to establish a culture that encourages effective communication. How often do people avoid meaningful dialogue for fear of conflict and failure? Proper, timely feedback is critical. Effective communication is honest, empathetic, accurate, frequent, and completed to real understanding.

Pass the Rock

Proper feedback is a critical element toward continuous improvement and goal attainment. In order to ensure an environment where every voice on the team is heard, Team Fastrax uses a simple technique called *Pass the Rock*. It works like this: the team sits down to debrief a training jump and they literally pass a rock from one person to the next. If you have the rock you are the ONLY person that can speak. No one else says a word while the person with the rock is expressing his or her opinion, and everyone makes an effort to respect each other's comments.

The typical feedback process will include what went well on the jump and where the team can improve, with emphasis on the training objectives for that specific jump. Once the rock is passed around the group and each person has had an opportunity to speak, the floor is open for comments and suggestions for improvement. By using a *Pass the Rock* method it ensures that no one person dominates the feedback process and that more soft-spoken people are given an opportunity to express themselves. An effective feedback system can become a very efficient accountability tool when there are relevant metrics in place

Accountability

We seek out success in its many forms on a never-ending quest to realize peak performance. Of course, there are as many definitions of success as there are people to give their opinion of it. An Olympic gold medal may be the defining moment for a team to claim success. Some people might claim success as well if they raise healthy, happy children.

However you choose to define success, accountability is a key element that allows us to modify our behavior in the interest of the goal. We are most effective when we have measurable key indicators that allow us to develop and maintain an established standard.

Through the United States Parachute Association, the skydiving industry keeps accurate records on jumper fatalities and injuries, which allows for critical adjustments to established student-training programs. Drop zones and instructors are held accountable to implement the changes that ensure a safe operation. We should foster a system of accountability in our organizations so we too can make critical adjustments to our business plan and keep the organization on track to land on target.

Measure performance
To further drive improvement, Team Fastrax very methodically measures individual and team performance on each jump. Like the total quality-management methods used in manufacturing, a competitive four-way team must become efficiency experts. Wasted time in transitions between formations means fewer points scored. Missed grips and errors also mean fewer points scored. Therefore, transition times and error rates become critical elements to measure and review for continuous improvements. By clearly establishing measurable objectives for the team and each person, we can hold each other accountable and further drive improvements.

Initiative

What are the motivating factors that might drive you to jump from an airplane in the first place? Some of these factors might include affiliation, achievement, or self-actualization. Or maybe you just want the "rush" that so many of us seek. The bottom line is that people are motivated for many reasons.

Often our lives seem like the life David Carradine confronts in the old *Kung Fu* television series. Life is a constant series of highs and lows, challenges, victories, and defeats. In order to deal with this in our organizations, it is necessary that we establish a culture that encourages personal initiative. Effective cultures allow people to be courageous and make adjustments to their activities when necessary. Most important is the willingness to take the critical jumps that represent some level of risk.

Commitment

Even if we recognize all these critical elements, is there a commitment to integrating them into the organization? We can clearly identify our destination, but the flight path for our parachutes often seems windy and uncertain, filled with other parachutes, trees, and various other obstacles. Will we have the persistence and determination to see things through? If we are not committed, our efforts will certainly falter in the face of adversity.

The Business Case for Good Communication

At one of the top communications consulting firms in Washington, D.C., the client list continues to grow based on word of mouth about the firm's superior client service. The firm is committed to clear and consistent communication, both as their ostensible business and in the way they serve their clients.

Client teams are formed regularly as new clients retain the firm's counsel. Depending on the size of the project or account, teams usually include one to two vice presidents (VPs) and two to three account managers (AMs).

However, traditional hierarchies change when account teams form: VPs can serve in supporting roles with an AM heading up the team, depending on the particular area of expertise required, as well as the work load and initiative of the staff. What remains the same is the process by which account teams form, assume roles and responsibilities, and carry out client business. (continued)

The account lead, whether the role is filled by someone senior or junior in the firm, preps the team, determines assignments, and leads meetings with the client. Each team member is accountable for his or her own deliverables, and the account lead trusts that assignments are completing to deadline unless she hears otherwise. Early in the week, an internal meeting serves to facilitate intra-team communications on the status of projects and any challenges that team members are facing. A weekly meeting with the client typically addresses strategy and tactics, and is followed up by memo to verify decisions and next steps. A weekly status report confirms assignment progress.

When necessary, the team hastens communications as events or issues require. Responsiveness, in addition to the regular sequence of weekly communications, fuels successful team dynamics and creates satisfied clients.

Be consistent

If you have taken the time to establish a foundation of commitment, then success often comes down to consistent, quality repetition. Whether you are a sales representative, purchasing agent, or loving parent, you must put forth consistent, quality repetition. One sure way to confuse the people around us is to expose them to confusing and inconsistent behavior, especially if you maintain a "do as I say, not as I do" pattern!

To help build consistency, identify the motivating factors for yourself and the people around you. Tap into that powerful source of commitment.

Leadership plays a critical role. Who can be a leader? The answer is each one of us can. We all can assume leadership roles by the example we set. I challenge you to make the jump.

Achieving Long-term Results

Once we have a healthy organizational culture and have taken the time to establish a clear vision, specific goals, and the related plan of action, how can we maintain our focus at this higher level of performance in a world of constant change and adversity? This whole process is a self-sustaining philosophy. If all the cells in the canopy are inflated and functioning properly, and all the suspension lines of organizational culture are intact, you are well positioned to deal with any shifts in the wind that might attempt to blow you off target. One final comment on sustaining successful efforts:

Keys to Making the Jump

An appropriate organizational culture supports the vision, goals, and action plans. The absence of any one of these will be detrimental to success.

The six elements of an appropriate organizational culture are trust, preparation, communication, accountability, initiative, and commitment.

Courageous Questions

Which of the six elements of a healthy culture are strong within your organization and which need improvement?

How will you help create the environment that builds the culture you desire?

Do you have these elements in place in your personal life? What will you do about it?

Selecting a Parachute Packer

The Value of Effective Hiring

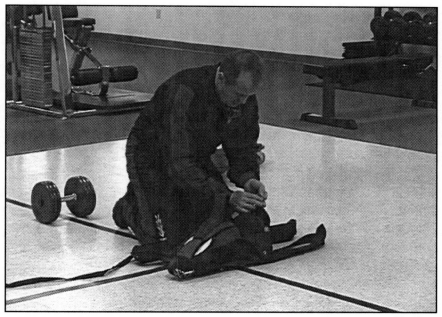

Kurt Loy

Packing a parachute at the Team Fastrax training facility.

There is a coming labor storm. Among many factors, the aging baby boomer population and a decrease in the technical-skilled applicant pool will drive a workforce shortage. Employee loyalty will continue to decrease and turnover will increase as the Generation X and Y workforce moves from one employer to the next, seeking career-development opportunities.

As all these applicants circulate through the recruiting process, this shift may cause some employers to lower their standards or shortcut an effective hiring process. This increase in job seekers will also circulate more undesirable applicants hiding a criminal history and poor work performance. How can employers ensure the effective placement of the right person in the right position?

First-hand Knowledge

If you were going to skydive, whom would you trust to pack your parachute? Would you be thorough in your selection process? Would you hire the lowest bidder? Most likely, you would feel more confident if you knew the packer had a history of competence, and took their time to ensure systematic and errorless packing. During my twenty-one years of parachuting and in 2,200 jumps, I have had five emergency situations that caused me to use my reserve or backup parachute. I'm alive because a thoroughly competent professional packed my reserve.

We're all packing each other's parachutes in our organizations. Our individual daily activities and interactions with others all contribute to the success of the organization.

Trust your packer
Much like driving your car frequently, if you do something like this long enough, a situation will arise. In skydiving an emergency situation leaves you with a rapid heart rate and might cause you to question the competence of your packer. The experience also makes you want to hug the person who

packed your backup parachute, which functioned properly and saved your life.

Should an emergency situation take place, there is a tradition in the sport that you reward the rigger who packed your reserve parachute with a gift of their favorite liquor, a well-earned reward indeed.

The Value of Effective Screening

There is a very real value associated with an effective hiring process in skydiving and in life. In business, estimated turnover costs are anywhere from one to three times an employee's annual salary. The expenses of recruiting, training, unproductive work from a poor hire, termination of employment, and then hiring a replacement add up very fast. Losing a top performer hurts even more.

Hard costs
It is expensive to make a bad hiring decision. If you hire someone with a criminal history and the employee commits a similar crime, you should be aware employers lose negligent hiring lawsuits 76 percent of the time, and the average lawsuit is $1.6 million dollars. However, let's not just focus on the negative; if we are effective in our hiring efforts and increase the quality of our workforce, we can significantly increase our organizational performance.

Alignment with Organizational Goals

To ensure that the hiring system is effective, employers should strive to create a hiring process that enables new employees to "buy into" the organizational goals and vision. Fully engaged employees are more productive than employees who don't fully understand what the organization is trying to accomplish and how they fit in. How many applicants have asked in the first interview, "Now what exactly is it you do here?" Not very encouraging is it? If they don't know what you do, how can they possibly know if the organization, let alone if the job, is a good fit for them? After the employee's initiative to learn, it's up to the employer to ensure they are fully aware of the corporate vision, goals, and how they fit in.

Would you jump?

As part of my speaking and training, Jump Institute will facilitate tandem skydives for the participants. Skydiving instructors are highly trained and experienced professionals, so very little training or action is required of the would-be first-time jumper. For some unknown reason, these people who are selected to jump will decline the offer because they can't "align" themselves with a goal that entails exiting an airplane from an altitude of two miles.

Like hiring a new employee, most people take this stance because they have not been properly educated. Alignment is likely when people are more fully informed regarding the "real" risks versus "perceived" ones, the excellent record of safety in the sport, and the instructor's personal competencies. These people are more likely to "step up," accept the challenge, and align themselves to taking the leap.

Ensuring Alignment

Karen manages a corporate recruiting department that employs skilled labor to install below-ground pipelines for various purposes. Most positions require the employees to spend a great deal of time exposed to the outdoor elements while operating heavy equipment. The job requirements are very physically demanding.

In an effort to ensure a proper new-hire fit and reduce expensive turnover, Karen implemented a "ride along program" as part of the hiring process. Basically, the applicant spends the better part of a day riding in the vehicle with existing employees. Doing this allows applicants to see the actual job requirements and work conditions. Typically the applicant can determine if the job is suitable for them or not. This also gives the existing employee opportunities to screen the applicant during the ride along.

The program significantly reduced terminations due to substandard employee performance, as well employees leaving because of poor job fit.

Be Systematic

As in packing a parachute, it is important to be systematic in the hiring process. By doing this, you are more likely to be legally compliant, and will minimize time and errors through frequent, correct repetition. How many steps are acceptable for your packer to miss in the packing process? Would you expect them to rush their work?

It is critical to be systematic in the hiring process. By doing this, you are more likely to be legally compliant, with minimal time and errors through frequent and correct repetition.

Stick to the system

How many front-line managers involved in your selection process have very little actual hiring training and don't fully understand the real cost associated with poor applicant screening and selection? As a result, do they often rely too heavily on gut instinct and rush through the selection process? In general, do they use a systematic and effective approach? An effective process places the right candidate in the right position, and aligns the new employee with the company vision and goals. In doing so, the new employee is more likely to be fully engaged and productive from day one.

Every individual we hire is an investment in the success of our organization. I challenge you to take a critical look at your hiring process.

Keys to Making the Jump

 Talent Pool: Maintain an effective level of quality and quantity in your potential talent pool of recruits. Avoid putting yourself in a position of desperation where you have limited options and possibly select the best of the worst.

 Identify "Must Haves": Take the time to clearly identify the specific requirements for success each position requires. "Must Haves" are those skills, abilities, and competencies that are never compromised and allow for easy identification of qualified applicants.

 Maintain Standards: While reviewing applications and resumes it is important to maintain the standards dictated by your organizational vision, goals, and action plans. Pay the price now or pay it later, but afterwards the implications of poor hiring decisions are likely to be much more expensive.

 Be Systematic: Effective packers minimize time and error through frequent and correct repetitions. Use the same fundamentals in your hiring practices—have a system and stick to it.

 Alignment: Ensure that both the organization and the recruit are in complete alignment with the culture and critical objectives. Hire the right people into the right organization and positions.

Courageous Questions

 Are you the right person in the right position within your organization? Did you feel that way when you were hired? If not, what brought about this change in your belief?

 Do you have the right people packing your parachute? If not, what do you intend to do about it? And when?

 How will you address the shortcomings in your hiring process? Be specific in stating what these shortcomings may be. Consider systematic solutions that encourage individuals' alignment with corporate goals.

Cut Away a Bad Canopy

Thoughts on Turnover and Retention

John Judy

*Team Fastrax uses extensive wind-tunnel
training to achieve peak performance.*

Get Them While They Are Hot

Being a skydiving instructor and having introduced hundreds of people to this exciting sport, I have noticed an interesting phenomenon. It occurs in both skydiving with new jumpers and in business once we hire new employees and they go through the initial blur of new-hire training. The new employee is quite often thrown into the fire and left to develop his or her own on-the-job training program.

In skydiving, it all starts when a first-time jumper is bitten by the "free-fall bug" and decides to make it a frequent activity. These new converts of the clouds are hungry for knowledge and eager to experience the many thrills of the sport. They move through the student program as efficiently as their time, money, and training will allow, and eventually graduate to non-student status.

You're hired

We call this process "on-boarding" in corporate America. After the student graduates, the typical drop-zone staff wishes him or her well and moves on to the next student who needs training. The newly minted skydiving school graduate has all the necessary skills to plummet through the sky in control of their bodies (albeit with the same wobbly consistency of a five-year-old who just got their bike's training wheels removed!), activate their own primary parachute at a safe altitude (very important!), handle any emergency situation that might arise (we hope!), and land without incident (maybe a grass stain here and there, but all limbs intact). After all this, they are off to explore the bigger and better aspects of the sport with more experienced skydivers.

The Awkward Gap

New skydivers quickly discover there is a huge gap in their skill level compared to the other jumpers who have had hundreds or even thousands of additional jumps to perfect their skills and abilities. These "newbie" skydivers find themselves in the same awkward place new employees do after they complete their initial orientation.

Who's going to help?

You can guess what happens next: none of the talented, experienced jumpers (sometimes called "Sky Gods," and not affectionately) want to play with the new rookies. This is the case unless one is an experienced jumper who is fundamentally generous and has a burning desire to work with up-and-coming student graduates (which can be very nerve-racking and has little to no financial incentive).

Frustration sets in

Frustrated with his or her lack of progression, the rookie becomes disheartened and leaves the sport to take up bowling, a sport with many more welcoming participants, and the opportunity to drink beer while enjoying the activity. In fact, this turnover of new jumpers is a very common occurrence in skydiving.

Sound similar to any organization for which you have worked? Have you ever seen a new hire that was, more or less, set up to fail? How can we keep that "home fire burning" in our new employees and direct them so that they are fully engaged in their work?

Burn Out

I've often observed a typical new employee show up for his or her first day of work with a high degree of personal motivation. Yet, as this person is exposed to the "harsh realities" of the business world, sometimes the proverbial fire can fade. In the worst-case scenario, the employee might turn into an unproductive pessimist. This phenomenon is more often than not a by-product of the established systems and culture within the organization, and not an intentionally malicious act on management's part. Nonetheless, the harm has been done.

Eventually the employee begins buying lottery tickets and prays to escape the drudgery of his or her daily activities, becomes less engaged in his or her work, and actively seeks employment elsewhere.

But alas, the grass is often not greener in the next pasture either, and anyone can find themselves on a similar treadmill of dread, complaining about how competitive the industry has become, how directionless the company is, and how unrewarding his or her daily activities remain. News Flash: Both the new hire and the organization have a role in avoiding these scenarios.

Fly Your Own Parachute

There is a saying that your attitude affects your altitude. In Stephen Covey's work *Seven Habits of Highly Effective People*, he discusses each person's "Circle of Influence." In a nutshell, Covey proposes that there are things we can control in life, such as our attitudes and activities, and some things we just cannot control, such as death, taxes, and weather patterns.

Our goal should be to expand our circle and gain additional control of our lives by not worrying about the things we can't control outside the circle and instead focusing on the things we can control inside the circle. More than anything, our attitude is the one thing over which we should work to gain greater control.

Individually, you can gain greater control of your circumstances by maintaining a positive attitude, directly addressing concerns with people (that means no complaining at the water cooler), and aggressively seeking opportunities to strengthen areas of weakness.

You have a leadership role in this outcome, so look for opportunities to strengthen relationships and network internally. When training opportunities arise, "leap" at them. Your attitude will remain positive and your circle of influence will expand like an opening parachute.

Mentoring: It's Not All About You

Everyone has a role in the retention of talented co-workers. The entire burden does not rest solely on the shoulders of management or solely the individual. Rather, everyone has a role in the outcome.

Much of the time, we go about our daily activities and don't fully realize the impact that we have (good and bad), on the people around us. Leaders can address this by frequent and open communication, by encouraging veteran employees to embrace new hires and mentor them in their progress. Creating an environment that encourages this necessary mentoring and training will help make the organization stronger and will have a profound positive effect on the turnover and retention of talent.

Keys to Making the Jump

On-boarding: Ensure an effective orientation program that ensures new employees get off on the right foot and are aligned with organizational goals.

Fly your own parachute: Take the initiative and be a source of positive influence in your organization.

Mentoring: Establish a mentoring program that allows new employees to learn from other veteran employees.

Courageous Questions

Are you losing talented people within your organization that you need to keep?

How will you retain the key players in your organization and what will motivate them to stay?

Do you provide the tools for employees to succeed within your organization?

Train Like a Skydiver

Effective Training and Coaching Within Organizations

Team Fastrax Select, an all-female team, listens to input from coach Niklas Hemlin.

Can you imagine making your first skydive with insufficient training and weak preparation? What a stressful plane ride up to jump altitude that would be! The fact is that every first-time jumper goes through extensive training prior to each jump to ensure that he or she is fully prepared. Early on in the student's progression, there is a great deal of time spent on the fundamentals. As he or she progresses in skill level, the student transitions from an intense focus on basic safety, to an emphasis on personal performance in advanced body and canopy flight.

We can increase organizational performance using the same principles that include an effective employee training and coaching program.

Start With the Basics

The consequences of failure in skydiving can be very serious and have a dramatic impact on your health. Tandem skydiving has an outstanding safety record and requires very little training on the student's part. The student is harnessed to a highly trained and experienced tandem instructor. Therefore, the instructor will handle any given situation, and probably more effectively than a student. If a student decides to progress in the sport beyond tandem jumping and become a qualified, experienced skydiver, he or she will need to jump alone, and handle any routine or emergency situation that may occur.

Safety first

In the skydiving student's progression there is a heavy emphasis on proficiency in the area of safety, and rightly so. To achieve proficiency, students are thoroughly trained and tested on the ground. Effective training is conducted in many ways to ensure that students can perform the basic safety procedures and operate the equipment. There should be no plane ride to altitude until students show they can perform the task on the ground, and there is no point in progressing to advanced tasks until they have mastered the competency of their current level.

If a student lacks the ability to demonstrate competence and becomes confused on the ground, what will happen when he or she is in free fall at 120 mph, and life depends on the ability to react quickly and properly to an emergency? The reality is that the student will likely respond to the level of his or her training and coaching; therefore, poor training equals poor performance.

New hires and promotions

When "on-boarding" employees or moving them to a new status or position within an organization, it is important that we start with the basics and build upon the fundamental requirements for the success the position requires. Like the typical skydiving student, employees will respond to any given situation to the level of their skills and ability.

An effective training program builds on the basics and inspires confidence and focus. In addition, dramatic increases in performance are realized when this training is conducted in conjunction with effective coaching. A competent coach will take the steps to identify strengths and weaknesses in an employee and ensure that the required information is presented at the appropriate skill level.

Student Progression

At some point, the student will be required to clearly demonstrate mastery of the basic safety procedures and other student proficiencies. Over many skydives he or she will be tested on things like free-fall stability, altitude awareness, ability to activate the main parachute, and ability to land safely.

To an experienced skydiver/instructor with thousands of successful skydives, the information appears to be very simple and straightforward. It can easily be taken for granted that the student can perform these when called upon to do so. From a student prospective, though, the information seems overwhelming and complex, and students likely question their ability to quickly identify a problem and react appropriately.

Put yourself in their shoes

For example, when the student pulls the main rip cord handle to activate the primary parachute, there is a complex decision tree of possible consequences, some good and some bad, and there is a related decision tree that dictates the appropriate response. A decision tree prescribes appropriate action for various situations. If x happens then respond by performing y. The best thing that can happen, and what every student is praying for, is that the main parachute opens properly and stops their rapid descent to *terra firma*.

Something can and might go wrong on a skydive. Having made thousands of skydives, I have experienced five emergencies that required me to activate my reserve or backup parachute. All these equipment malfunctions were different, but all of them were handled by a predetermined procedure. The procedure allowed me to react quickly to each situation.

It would be irresponsible to allow a skydiving student to progress in the sport without mastering the basics first. Why should our organizations be any different?

An effective coach identifies an appropriate training progression. In the best-case scenario, individuals are coached and trained to move up to the next skill level or position.

Poor Training Equals Poor Performance

In the absence of real-time feedback, how will people respond to any given situation? Often we revert to past experiences, old habits, and training. There are many combinations of scenarios that can arise on any given skydive. However, there is a basic decision tree of actions that a skydiver can utilize and follow to decide on the best course of action.

Prepare to respond appropriately
An effective training system will prepare the student to respond correctly to many and varied possible scenarios. Proper training and preparation give the student a sense of confidence and focus. Conversely, poor training can leave the student overly stressed and distracted—not a good thing in free fall.

As with skydiving students, new and existing employees are typically highly motivated to learn, and for good reason—their professional success depends on it. Unbelievably, some students are overconfident and can give the coach or instructor a false sense of their full understanding, making it hard to determine if they can perform properly when called upon to do so. For this reason, students must be thoroughly tested to ensure full comprehension and proper execution.

Higher Learning

Get the basics right first

It is important to note that you can accelerate students to become world-class formation-skydiving athletes, but you cannot do it without getting the basics right first.

Looking back at my progression in the sport, it's hard to remember how it felt to be a student over twenty years ago. Most experienced skydivers with a few thousand jumps achieve a high level of comfort in free fall and, in fact, put the vast majority of their focus during any given skydive on advancing their body- and canopy-flight skills. The basic equipment operation and procedures become second nature. A competitive athlete in formation skydiving cannot afford to allocate wasted mental energy on basic skydiving procedures.

Push the limits

The successful skydiving competitor will consistently introduce new theories, alternative perspectives, and knowledge into their training progression. In fact, most people desire to be professionally challenged and developed and welcome the opportunity to expand their knowledge and capabilities. I challenge you to look within your organizations and determine if you have an effective training program that promotes increasing levels of knowledge and performance.

Training is Rewarding

Lisa, an executive with a Midwest-based credit union, had this to say about the value of an effective training program. "Within our credit union we rely heavily on our employees to do the right thing, making the right decisions on a daily basis. Our emphasis on training has never been of greater importance. Developing our workforce and future leadership is the secret to our sustained success.

"Ongoing training challenges high performers, our key assets. This is essential to elongating his or her career with the credit union. This is also essential to avoiding workforce burn out and reduces further turnover. Personal and professional development and promoting from within is rewarding for our employees and a cost-effective investment for the organization.

We have found that consistency in training appropriate skills and abilities is critical. Career-oriented programs are attended on a regular basis, including ongoing new-hire, internal-system, and financial investment training—all are equally important to achieving our goals. Ideally, every wheel in the machine is greased properly for optimum efficiency and effectiveness, ensuring peak performance.

On Coaching

It makes good business sense to accelerate the learning by using the best resources and training tools available at the time. Coaching is a tool that can yield tremendous results and significantly shorten the learning curve.

Effective coaching can be used in nearly all aspects of life. Coaching has obvious implications in sports; a great coach can make or break an athletic team. Within any given organization, we can often find the resources we might need. However, if this is required, we must also be willing to look outside our organizations to achieve the results desired and to accelerate the performance curve.

Bronze medal champions
A great example of this is Team Fastrax. Within a two-year period, starting in late 2002, the team went from an unknown recreational team to an internationally competitive team.

A significant factor in the team's success has been the willingness to use performance accelerators, including world-class technical-skydiving coaches, sports psychologists, nutritionists, extensive wind-tunnel training, and thousands of training and competition jumps.

World-class skydiving coach Niklas Hemlin, Swedish national champion, became a competitor and a coach for the team early on in the project. Because of his deep technical knowledge and experience, the team was able to quickly explore performance-enhancing options and have a successful role model to imitate.

Business implications
An effective coach deeply understands the subject matter and has the ability to present it in a way that each person can understand. Sometimes it takes repeated exposure over time to the same information before someone fully comprehends the message and embraces it. This aids in overcoming the

challenges of various learning styles and accelerates the learning process.

Continuous Improvement

The history of parachuting is a story of courage, daring, innovation, and persistence. At some point, skydivers began holding onto each other in free fall. As the skill levels increased during the 1980s and 1990s, people began to experiment with building large, choreographed formations. Eventually, a 100-person formation was built, then 200 people, and then more than 300 people linked in free fall. Like many great feats and milestones, what was once thought impossible is now considered routine.

Rapid early progression

The improvements along the learning curve for this progression happened over decades of continuous innovation and pushing widely accepted boundaries and limiting beliefs. One thing that becomes evident during a skydiver's progression is the huge leaps in performance that take place early on in their progression. If a student progresses to the point of being a world-class athlete in formation skydiving, the improvements are incrementally smaller and require much more effort to achieve. This is much like an Olympic swimmer or track athlete who is training to shave fractions of a second off his or her lap times.

Consistent and effective training are necessary requirements for an environment of continuous improvement.

Training Versus Competing

A formation-skydiving team may spend one to three hours in preparation for every thirty-five to sixty seconds of actual free fall, and in fact may make hundreds if not a thousand jumps training for ten to thirty competition jumps over the course of a year.

This is prevalent throughout business as well. For example, how much time does a sales rep actually spend in front of a client on a sales call, versus the amount of time he or she spends in preparation? During the average forty-hour work week, he or she most likely spends a small percentage of their time in front of clients closing deals. Much more of his or her time is spent in preparation and the related follow-up afterward.

Return on training
Disciplined training and the appropriate level of coaching are required to sustain growth and performance. In hard times, it is not uncommon for corporate training to take a back seat or become a low priority. The irony is that training is likely most called for when times are tough. Some might view this as a misuse of resources in an organization; others will view it as an investment in future returns.

Hire Motivated People

For the same reasons that skydivers use it, training and coaching is a critical component of any high-performance organization. It has proven more effective to hire someone who has the fundamental motivation and character required but needs skills training. This is opposed to hiring someone who possesses a high skill level but is not self-motivated.

Can you imagine the futility of ground training and drilling safety procedures with a student who has absolutely no intention of ever skydiving? The entire process would be a pointless exercise, frustrating for both the student and the coach. Yet a sincere and motivated student, working hard with a qualified and experienced coach, will likely master the required skills with commitment and practice.

They have to want to jump

An organization can always train someone to acquire and practice the skills required for a position. It is much harder, if not impossible, to instill motivation and character. The desired performance has roots in employee motivation, nurtured by the investment of coaching and committed hours of practice for the moment of a perfect landing. When this happens, you know you have trained like a skydiver.

An organization can always train someone to acquire and practice the skills required for a position. It is much harder, if not impossible, to instill motivation and character.

Keys to Making the Jump

🪂 Start with the basics; don't attempt to push progress at the expense of a solid foundation of knowledge.

🪂 Put yourself in the student's shoes; what seems basic to you might be quite complex and difficult to grasp for someone newly exposed to the information.

🪂 Poor training equals poor performance. We had a saying in the Rangers: "More sweat in training, less blood in combat."

🪂 Always be a student; constantly expand your mind with new theories, techniques, and thoughts.

🪂 Coaching is critical and can rapidly accelerate a team to success.

Courageous Questions

🪂 In what areas could you effectively use coaching for yourself?

🪂 Is your training program in line with your organizational goals? Are people prepared for success?

🪂 Do you foster an environment of continuous improvement? How can you enhance this area?

🪂 How can you improve upon the current coaching and mentoring that is taking place within your organization? Do you have the ability to bring someone else along?

Fly the Parachute

The Role of Leadership in High-Performance Teams

Anna Ferguson

Team Fastrax members Bob Akers and David Hart pilot their canopies to land on target at an event.

Strong leadership is a key element in all great teams and organizations. Leadership is a competency that has been analyzed, dissected, researched, and documented from just about every perspective imaginable. Well, here's one more perspective—a skydiver's.

Imagine that the parachute itself represents the members or components of a team, the suspension lines that connect the parachute and the jumper are the culture, and the jumper is the leadership involved in landing the parachute on target. The jumper picks the spot to exit the plane, taking into account the intended landing target. The jumper deploys the main parachute, and then, using two steering toggles, pilots the parachute to land on target.

Just as in landing a parachute on target with consistency, there is no substitute for experience when developing leadership skills.

Someone Has to Steer

The jumper represents the formal leadership in the organization—holding the toggles to the parachute, guiding and controlling the parachute to land on target. This is the person who holds a management position and wields formal power and influence. He or she is called upon to make strategic or tactical decisions on a daily basis.

Pack your parachute
An effective leader ensures that his or her parachute is packed properly BEFORE boarding the aircraft. The proper selection of teammates is a critical first step to landing on target. These

teammates, as cells of the main canopy, must all perform as required when called upon to do so.

The suspension lines connecting the main canopy to the jumper are the critical elements of a healthy culture. Effective leadership ensures these suspension lines of trust, commitment, accountability, preparation, initiative, and communication are in place. It is the leader's constant challenge to facilitate a culture in which each of these areas is properly represented.

Keep your cool

An effective canopy pilot is not overly reactive with erratic toggle input to overcompensate for obstacles on the ground and changing wind conditions. More often than not, this type of behavior is counterproductive and wastes energy. By the same token, if the jumper is too intimidated to fly the parachute or hasn't had the proper coaching or training, he or she will allow the canopy to fly itself and pray to land on target and not get hurt in the process.

Don't be a control freak

Leadership within organizations is very much the same process; too much micromanagement can lead to frustration and low initiative within the team. Too little input and interaction can lead to low accountability, weak goal focus, and, ultimately, poor results. Effective leadership includes the ability to balance all the relevant critical factors to land on target.

Informal Leadership

A great deal of influence exists outside the senior-management structure in organizations and in teams. The workforce of an organization can have a dramatic influence on the tactical and strategic direction taken. In fact, some might argue that the real power lies within the informal element and outside the corner offices.

Frontline knowledge and experience

The people who are in the trenches living, breathing, and sweating the everyday challenges often see the "reality" of the situations where "the rubber meets the road." At its best, a management team solicits ongoing feedback from all levels to adjust and land on target. Influence is wielded when the workforce collaborates to address challenges and arrive at solutions.

Inspire Jumps

Innovation and continuous improvement often require courageous jumps; effective leadership establishes an enabling culture of trust that builds the necessary confidence and drives success, which in turn drives confidence. Leadership inspires the proverbial leap required in a high-performance organization.

First-jump confidence

How can you inspire these leaps? Skydiving instructors make a special effort to build confidence and trust with a first-jump student. This is done through effective training, coaching, and informing the student about the "real" risks and rewards of skydiving. The instructor will also instill understanding about the reliability of the equipment and the student's ability to operate it. A critical role of effective leadership is to establish this culture of trust and sincere confidence that comes from thorough training and appropriate coaching.

Communicate Understanding

During my enlistment as an Airborne Ranger, it became apparent there were two primary activities that consume a Ranger's time. These two activities separate into the realities that either you are in actual combat or you are training and preparing for combat. As a competitive skydiver, either you are in competition or you are training and preparing for competition.

The fact is that the vast majority of time is spent in preparation and training for the main event. The effectiveness of this training is reflected in the results when the Ranger unit is deployed to actual combat or a competition skydiving team competes. Leadership plays a critical role in the ultimate success or failure throughout training and competition by their ability to communicate effectively.

Ranger mission briefings

In the Rangers, prior to every mission it is the role of an effective leader to clearly communicate the objective of the mission, the action plan, and each person's role within the parameters of the planned mission. The Ranger mission planning session can be quite lengthy and covered in great detail.

Successful missions most often begin with a good plan, one that is effectively communicated and well understood by everyone. In competitive skydiving, jump preparation is equally important. It quickly becomes apparent when a four-way team has not properly prepared for a skydive; the team execution is erratic and confused, and ultimately, the team underperforms. In every team environment, someone must step forward to ensure effective communication takes place and that everyone understands his or her role.

Failure Drives Improvement

Teams will make mistakes, under perform, have setbacks, and yes, sometimes fail. An effective leader recognizes that failure drives improvement and establishes an environment where the team can push their performance to higher levels and learn from failures.

Solicit constant feedback

This is most often done through an effective feedback process. Consider the "live fire" exercises that Ranger units use quite extensively to simulate combat and drive an increase in performance. During my enlistment in the First Ranger Battalion, our company commander mentioned a statistic that our 120-man Ranger Company expended more live ammunition in training in six months than the entire Twenty-Fourth Infantry Division did in the same twelve-month calendar year. Needless to say, we trained extremely hard and in as realistic to combat conditions as possible. In this environment, things will sometimes go wrong and people will make mistakes.

A close call

In one particular "live fire" exercise, I recall assaulting an objective with my fire team while a support element covered our assault from a distance, firing automatic weapons onto the objective. Through miscommunication, the support element didn't notice the "lift and shift" signal to move the supporting fire off the objective as my team assaulted the targets. This significant error did not become apparent until my five-man assault team was standing on the objective as a blizzard of bullets snapped by our bodies at supersonic speed and chunks of nearby trees exploded from the impact of bullets.

Learn from your mistakes

In cases like this, when time distorts and seconds seem like an eternity, the error was identified when we threw ourselves to the ground and a "cease fire" was called. The point is that even an elite unit trained to a razor's edge is always pushing the limits, and mistakes will happen. Fortunately, no one was hurt and it created an incredible learning experience for everyone, the details of which were revealed in comprehensive after-action review. After-action reviews—used extensively in the military—drive continuous improvement and require a setting where everyone can express his or her perspective on what was good and bad, and how to improve.

> **Effective 360-degree feedback and healthy conflict is a sign of a team pushing for improvements and innovation.**

Strong Leadership Sets the Tone, Inside and Outside of the Company

After accounting improprieties were discovered and reported, the U.S. subsidiary of an international parent company needed strong leadership to build a new corporate culture and to lead the company's many operating divisions.

The parent company hired an industry-seasoned CEO who wasted no time in establishing a culture of integrity by replacing most of the senior management and by creating the new position of Chief Ethics and Compliance Officer (CECO). The CECO developed an ethics training program—the first development curriculum to roll out corporate-wide and into the divisions, most of which were companies that had been acquired and which operated independently. The next newly created position focused on safety, again engaging all segments of the organization in the program. (continued)

In these two key hires alone, the CEO sent a strong message about the company's uncompromising values of ethical conduct and the safety of its people. The initiatives inspired employees, many of whom had previously lost both faith in management and pride in their work. In addition, ethics and safety became the backbone of the company's marketing messages, distinguishing it among competitors in the industry.

A Culture of Improvement

An effective leader creates a culture of improvement, one in which the unvarnished truth is confronted in order to drive improvement. Egos and judgmental attitudes have no place in a healthy feedback process. A typical Team Fastrax training day may include twenty to forty training jumps. Every jump is thoroughly debriefed as a team to drive improvements.

It is important to realize that the leadership necessary to ensure a culture of improvement does not rest solely on the shoulders of the formal leadership. Every person on the team will, at one time or another, step forward and ensure that the team holds itself accountable to the standards it has identified for itself. Within organizations, that leadership can just as easily come from the lowest positions as it can a formal management position. It is everyone's responsibility to ensure that there is a culture where this can take place.

Keys to Making the Jump

🦅 Both formal and informal leadership plays a role in the success of a team.

🦅 Building a culture of confidence will inspire courageous leaps in innovation and continuous improvement. Communicate to real understanding in order to build confidence.

🦅 A failure often drives improvement; reward risk taking where appropriate and solicit effective feedback.

Courageous Questions

🦅 What role do you play as a leader within your organization?

🦅 How can you take personal responsibility and initiative to help the organization achieve its vision and goals?

🦅 What are you waiting for?

Choose Your Altitude

Effectively Confronting Obstacles and Challenges

John Judy

*A tandem-skydiving student takes the
leap with Team Fastrax.*

"To get profit without risk, experience without danger, and reward without work is as impossible as it is to live without being born." President Harry Truman

Taking the Leap

Before the jump

Being a skydiving instructor and having introduced hundreds of people to the exciting sport of skydiving, I have noticed an interesting behavior pattern in first-time jumpers. Students often tell me that their anxiety level (sometimes called terror) peaks when the aircraft door opens two miles high, the cool air of the higher altitude thunders inside the aircraft, and the "moment of truth" is upon them. Their last step out the door of the plane is a blur of sensation and emotion that flashes by in a gut-wrenching instant. Accelerating away from the safe confines of the plane and surrendering to gravity, the sixty-second free fall is a surreal experience of high-altitude beauty, heart-pounding adrenaline, and freedom.

After the jump

Conversely, upon being delivered safely to the ground by their parachute, students most often experience a state of euphoria, elation, and an intense sense of achievement. The experience provides a sweet reward for which no words or video can do justice. Like skydiving, having the courage to step outside our "comfort zone" and take appropriate risks in life and business can have a dramatic effect on our lives and on those of the people around us. Ultimately our attitudes have a dramatic effect on the very performance of the organizations we work for. Making "life jumps" is often the catalyst that drives our attitudes and our ability to soar to "higher altitudes" of success.

Jump!

It's Not the Fall That Kills You....

There's a joke in skydiving, "It's not the fall that kills you, it's the sudden stop at the end," and so it is in life and business. Attitude affects every aspect of our lives, even the bottom-line profitability of our organizations. Many companies have made the ultimate stop and gone out of business. Certainly the lack of workforce engagement plays no small part in these catastrophic failures.

The Gallup organization conducted extensive research on attitudes toward work and found that twenty-two million Americans are "actively disengaged" in their work; they are not only unhappy, but these people act out their feelings and actively undermine their co-workers.

The value of engagement

There are estimates that disengaged workers cost corporate America $300 billion a year. Some surveys show that an astonishing 65 percent of people said that they received no recognition for their good work in the last year. In most cases the number-one reason people quit jobs is because they don't feel appreciated.

We have a much more profound impact on each other's attitudes than we often realize, and the related impact to organizational profitability is significant. Let's take a closer look at how we can gain greater control of our attitudes in our daily lives.

Why Jump From a Perfectly Good Airplane?

We all have our own personal comfort zones, outside of which are a great deal of real and/or perceived risks. You wouldn't be unusual if a leap from a perfectly good airplane is not on your list of acceptable or even rational activities. I like to tell people, "If they were perfectly good airplanes they wouldn't have invented parachutes." However, we can all take lessons from the experience of skydiving. The simple act of actually getting outside your comfort zone so that you can drive positive personal growth and change requires a basic level of confidence, trust, and faith. It involves taking risks with no guarantee of success.

We are capable of great things if we only make the effort. If you do what you've always done, you'll get what you always got, right? The American lawyer and poet Eugene Ware wrote, "All glory comes from daring to begin." To cause meaningful change we have to "jump" outside our comfort zones.

Altitude Is Your Friend

The factors that drive our behavior are often complex and varied; however, we are all universally striving to live fulfilling, happy lives. Our ability to do this effectively is directly tied to our attitude. The following graph illustrates how attitude increases altitude, altitude being the measure of success.

Jump!

On the one axis are the "positive" attitude drivers—the behavior that takes a person to higher and safer altitudes. On the horizontal axis are the "negative" drivers that drag a person down emotionally and cause a person to lose altitude. The more intense the gravity of the negative behavior, the more your altitude decreases. Obviously, altitude in skydiving is a good thing. Lack of it can lead to catastrophic results. Professional boxer Sugar Ray Robinson said, "I've always believed that you can think positive just as well as you can think negative." Clearly, increasing positive behavior increases your effectiveness in life.

Attitude Increases Altitude

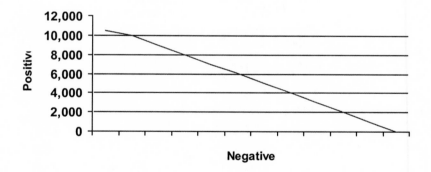

Make the "JUMP"

Follow this simple acronym called "JUMP" to fuel positive attitudes and gain altitude. Imagine you are eating a special pill for each letter in the word JUMP. Each pill empowers you to take leaps and follow these steps:

Just Pick One
Undo the Past
Mind Over Matter
Predict the Future

Just pick one thing and get started now

Don't try to accomplish too much at once; just pick one thing you will change right now. In order to stay effectively focused on your objective, it is critical to limit the amount of balls you have in the air at one time.

During my enlistment in the army, it became clear that the military generally considers a factor of four to be an acceptable number to focus on. In the military chain of command, you will rarely find more than four direct reports to any one individual. Through the rigors of intense combat it has been determined that this is the limit on which someone can intensely stay focused. You might consider using this factor when setting your major goals.

Undo the past

As soon as we meet another person, we begin to form an opinion, sometimes good and sometimes bad. Over time, we can hold onto a great deal of unproductive negative thoughts and feelings, including anger and resentment. Our feelings may be based on misunderstanding and poor communication, not reality.

As is often the case, we need to let go of the past to move forward into the future. This directly relates to our ability to communicate effectively within our organizations, as well as to our ability to open our minds to new possibilities. We must discard the past to move forward into the future.

Mind over matter—Make the commitment

Like it or not, we all carry around a limiting belief system about what we can or can't do. These beliefs are most often based on our perceptions and not realities. Anais Nin wrote, "We don't see things as they are, we see them as we are." Break your limiting beliefs of what you can and cannot do to free your attitude toward positive behavior. Make the mental commitment to get things started.

Predict the future

As do many competitive athletes, skydivers use imagery to enhance performance. Prior to each jump, I close my eyes and imagine the skydive in minute detail. I can feel the wind on my body, my teammates' jumpsuits, the flawless execution of the dive sequence, and the powerful feeling of success at the end of the dive. In effect, I predict a successful future in my mind before I ever do it.

Try this exercise in some aspect of your life where the importance of the outcome is high. Just close your eyes and imagine the outcome you desire in intense detail.

"Impossible" Challenges Require "Possible" Thinking

After September 11, 2001, the president and founder of a highly regarded adventure travel company met with his management team to discuss business strategy in the wake of the terrorist events. There was no shortage of gloomy predictions: people will be afraid to fly; vacations will seem frivolous in the face of war; people will want to be with their families, not out "adventuring." Never one to be limited by circumstance, the company's leader challenged the team to predict a better future for both the company and the entire travel industry.

Over the ensuing weeks, with cancellations pouring in, the team worked around the clock to keep the company afloat. Painful business decisions needed to be made. Yet the president remained positive and began to send inspiring personal messages to potential travelers and staff alike: "You and your family will always be a part of our family," "The wildness of nature is a soul-stirring antidote for man's inhumanity to man," "Let us embrace these values together," etc. Heartened by these ideas over the course of months, the staff agreed to salary reductions and office space constrictions, and previous travelers began to think in the long term and make plans—many with their families and extended families in order to gather and to heal. (continued)

By genuinely appealing to the human need to congregate and to find meaning in the wake of a tragedy, the president struck an enduring chord that bonded people to the company indelibly. That alone makes for a remarkable turnaround story. But this leader's vision was even more extraordinary—he collaborated with like-minded competitors in sending messages to customers and the media, both of which were transfixed on pessimistic travel news. Ultimately, his impetus developed into a groundswell and together with the healing effects of time, the travel industry recovered.

What If Something Goes Wrong?

I have some good and bad news for all would-be jumpers. First, the bad news: Although a remote possibility, something could possibly go wrong on any given skydive. The good news is that if things do go wrong, you'll have the rest of your life to think about it. I know: that's not funny, right? Yet I've had five emergencies where things did go wrong. I obviously dealt with each situation effectively or I wouldn't be writing this book.

Adversity is likely
Let me assure you that if you do anything frequently enough, you will have to deal with many intense crises and challenges. In the midst of you still have choices to make; choices that are within your control. Like the decisions I've made while skydiving that saved my life five times, you can choose your response to most any given situation in life. By controlling your attitude, you effectively choose your altitude.

Open your mind and jump
Remember, minds are like parachutes; they only function properly when open. When opportunities arise to have a positive impact on other people, "JUMP"! Your positive attitude is contagious. You will see your circle of influence expand like an opening parachute, and your life will soar to new altitudes. In the words of Abraham Lincoln, "Most people are about as happy as they make up their minds to be." Be courageous and "chose your altitude"!

Keys to Making the Jump

   Just Pick One: Don't attempt to bite off more than you can effectively chew. Use the factor of four to determine how many goals to focus on.

   Undo the Past: Let go of the past, including any anger, resentment, and limiting beliefs. These things only serve to hold you back.

   Mind Over Matter: We typically have more control over our own destiny than we perceive. Make up your mind to make it a good future.

   Predict the Future: The mind is a powerful thing; use it to its full potential. Create your own future using visualization and imagery.

Courageous Questions

   How can your organization foster a "Choose Your Altitude" work environment?

   Pick one thing you will change today in your personal life and within your organization.

About the Author

David Hart, a national speaker, writer, trainer, and former U.S. Army Ranger, leads the Jump Institute. He brings his unique experiences gained through decades of parachuting to each client engagement. He has jumped from as high as 21,000 feet, as low as 800 feet, and has made 100 skydives in just thirteen hours. David has thousands of parachute jumps completed to date, has competed at the U.S. Nationals several times, and has jumped out of cargo airplanes, hot-air balloons, helicopters, and even off bridges and into many high-profile events including NASCAR races, NCAA football games, and symphony performances. A graduate of the University of Cincinnati, David combines this experience with a solid grounding in business, having accumulated more than fifteen years of experience in sales, management, and marketing, including over five years as founder and CEO of a national retail/amusement company. David has written and been the subject of various articles and is the author of *JUMP! Leaps in Organizational Effectiveness and Teamwork.*

About Jump Institute

Vision:
We offer learning opportunities and services that educate and inspire people to action. Based on powerful skydiving-related metaphors, our insightful seminars, in-depth training sessions, and comprehensive supporting materials will stimulate organizations to action, and ultimately help facilitate meaningful increases in your organizational effectiveness and performance.

Look within. Leap beyond.℠

Products/Services:
Organizations utilize the Jump Institute to improve recruiting and retention, strengthen organizational effectiveness, and optimize their teams through the following products/services:

- Teamwork training and experiential learning sessions;
- Keynote, open-enrollment, and general-session presentations;
- Books and facilitator guides; and
- Team Fastrax-hosted events including demonstration jumps and tandem skydives.

Some Past Clients:
National Association of Church Business Administration (NACBA); Chambers of Commerce; Society of Human Resource Management (SHRM); International Paper/XPEDX; The Ohio University; Washington State College; Nestle Purina; Universal 1 Credit Union; YMCA; Jasper Engine and Transmission; American Society for Training & Development (ASTD); Ohio West Virginia Truckers Association; and many others.

Lisa Flory

A corporate group poses with Team Fastrax. Train with Team Fastrax to experience and develop peak performance that will encourage your team to look within and leap beyond.

For information on keynote presentations, team-building training, demonstration jumps, and other Jump Institute programs, contact us at:

Headquarters:
Jump Institute
3091 West Galbraith Road Suite 308
Cincinnati, Ohio 45239

Phone: (800) 325-3609 ext. 3088
Fax: (513) 728-4415
Email: *dhart@jumpinstitute.com*
Website: *www.jumpinstitute.com*

NATIONAL SPEAKERS ASSOCIATION